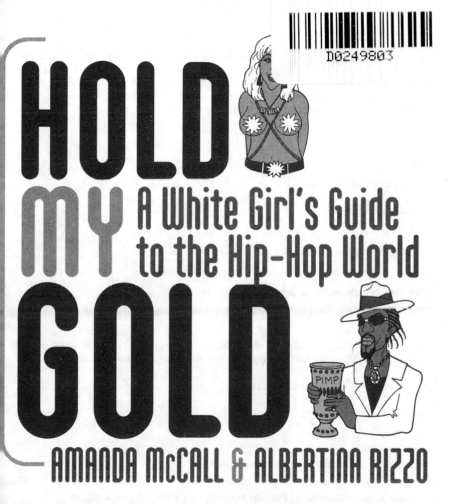

HOLD MY GOLD

A White Girl's Guide to the Hip-Hop World

AMANDA McCALL & ALBERTINA RIZZO

SIMON & SCHUSTER PAPERBACKS

New York London Toronto Sydney

DISCLAIMER: This is a work of fiction. Although certain real people are mentioned in the book, including Fat Joe, Ol' Dirty Bastard, Snoop Dog, Lil' Kim, Lil Jon, Eminem, and Kingpin Skinny Pimp, they are used ficticiously. In addition, none has authorized, approved of, or sponsored this book or otherwise participated in its preparation or publication and most likely believe that its authors are wack.

SIMON & SCHUSTER
Rockefeller Center
1230 Avenue of the Americas
New York, NY 10020

First Simon & Schuster trade paperback edition 2005

SIMON & SCHUSTER PAPERBACKS and colophon are registered trademarks of Simon & Schuster, Inc.

For information about special discounts for bulk purchases,please contact Simon & Schuster Special Sales at 1-800-456-6798 or business@simonandschuster.com

Designed by Joel Avirom and Jason Snyder

Manufactured in the United States of America

10 9 8 7 6 5 4 3 2 1

Library of Congress Cataloging-in-Publication Data

McCall, Amanda, 1980–
    Hold my gold : a white girl's guide to the hip-hop world / Amanda McCall & Albertina Rizzo.
      p.   cm.
    1. Youth. 2. Hip-hop. 3. Race relations. I. Rizzo, Albertina, 1976– II. Title.
HQ796.M3843 2005
305.2352'089'09073—dc22   2004062628

ISBN 0-7432-6460-6

DEDICATION

We dedicate this book to Andre 3000 and Big Boi
of Outkast with the hope that doing so will inspire
either them or their representatives to contact us
immediately to set up a meeting or a romantic
rendezvous.

HOLD MY GOLD*

* *A phrase often yelled by a young woman prior*
  to a fight. By asking someone to hold her gold, she
  is preventing her jewelry from being sullied or bloodied.
  While often meant as a challenge to "bitches who are
  frontin'," for the white girl, "hold my gold" is a symbolic
  battle cry in the war against her own lameness.
  This book, white girls, is your sword . . . use it mightily.

CONTENTS

INTRODUCTION: Chicken Soup for the White Girl

The word "CRUNK" (from the Latin "crunkus") can be loosely defined as "good feelings resulting from, or relating to, alcohol, gold, luxury goods, large breasts and buttocks, rare gems, boisterous noises, and gyration."

The word "WACK" (from the Latin "whitus maximus") is defined as "bad feelings resulting from, or relating to, brussels sprouts, John Tesh, herpes, polka, root canals, Beanie Baby collections, quicksand, flat tires, knitting circles, and kidney stones."

As a white girl living in a hip-hop world, you may

experience feelings of insecurity about your own bootyliciousness, feelings of unworthiness, uselessness. You may feel too inadequate to straddle a pole in a Jay-Z video, or feel lonely when everyone else at da club is drinking Cristal and you are on your second bottle of Amstel Light.

You've tried everything to make yourself less wack and, with every desperate attempt, you feel even lamer than when you started. You keep repeating the same mistakes over and over again: You go to a record store determined to buy the new Lil Jon CD and always leave with another John Tesh:

Live at Red Rocks

cassette tape. You head out to buy a forty oz. of Olde English "800" Malt Liquor and always return home with the same 1.5 ounce container of Twining's English Breakfast Tea. You become frustrated and want to give up. You begin to wonder whether you will ever overcome your wackness or if all white girls are destined to remain wack for the rest of their lives.

Well, white girl, you may be convinced that your pimp cup is half empty, but we're here to tell you that it's half full and the Hennessy is sweet. It is time for you to grab hold of your gem-encrusted destiny! In buying this book, you have already taken the first and perhaps most important step: Acknowledging that that which is mad white is also mad wack. Next, you must acknowledge that you are not alone.

Wackness among white girls ages thirteen to twenty-seven and a half has reached epidemic proportions. Recent statistics are shocking. Studies show that one in three white girls cries herself to sleep every night listening to Ludacris, wishing she could be part of that Cristal-soaked hip-hop dream. In Iowa and New Hampshire alone, more than 45 percent of

AMANDA McCALL & ALBERTINA RIZZO

white girls were admitted to emergency rooms between March 2001 and November 2004 for wackness-related injuries, most of which, hospital records show, can be attributed to the misguided pursuit of dangerous endeavors such as pole-straddling and

attempts at gyrating on the hood of moving vehicles. These kinds of tragic but preventable accidents can lead to both physical and, more importantly, emotional trauma, one that doctors have recently defined as W.I.D. or Wackness-Induced

Depression. Though recent research has shown that W.I.D. may be a genetic illness and not entirely curable, psychologists believe that, through a combination of behavioral therapy and a high consumption of expensive champagne, the illness *is* treatable.

Please take a moment to answer the following questions to determine whether you, like millions of other white girls, are suffering from W.I.D.

SELF-QUIZ: ARE YOU EXPERIENCING WACKNESS-INDUCED DEPRESSION (W.I.D.)?

1 *Little interest or pleasure in taking part in activities such as kayaking, skimming through J. Crew catalogs, or listening to Phish bootlegs.*

YES _____ NO _____

2 *In the last four weeks, you have experienced sudden feelings of fear or panic when looking in the mirror and realizing how wack you are.*

YES _____ NO _____

3 *Nausea or an upset stomach, or feel like you are going to have diarrhea when you realize your boyfriend is the spitting image of Ryan Seacrest.*

YES _____   NO _____

4 *Feel down, depressed, or hopeless about your ability to gyrate on the hood of a Cadillac Escalade.*

YES _____   NO _____

5 *Feel tired or have little energy to gyrate on the hood of a Cadillac Escalade.*

YES _____   NO _____

AMANDA McCALL & ALBERTINA RIZZO

6 *Feel badly about yourself or feel that you are a failure after watching a rap video.*

Yes _____ No _____

7 *Think that you would be better off dead, or want to hurt yourself in some way, for not owning a set of gold teeth.*

Yes _____ No _____

If you answered yes to three or more of these questions, you are suffering from W.I.D. and must immediately begin to de-wack. Congratulations, bitches!

Da Twelve Steps:

Wackness is a rough word to deal with. It can hit anyone. Polls indicate that wackness-induced lameness in America has tripled since 1981. A 2004 study indicates that over 92 percent of all Americans suffer from moderate to severe wackness. Some people live for years without even knowing how lame they actually are.

For those of you who have acknowledged your wackness, know that there IS help. With *Hold My Gold* as your Higher Power, you can turn your life around.

Before you begin this book, please review the following twelve steps. Each is crucial in beginning your journey to wackovery:

1   We admitted we were powerless over whiteness and that our wackness had become unmanageable.

2   Came to believe that a Power greater than ourselves (i.e., *Hold My Gold: A White Girl's Guide to the Hip-Hop World*) could restore our crunkness.

3   Made a decision to turn our will and our lives over to the care of this Girl's Guide.

4   Made a searching and fearless inventory of our clothing and accessories.

5   Admitted to a life-sized poster of Lil Jon, to ourselves, and to others the exact nature of our wackness.

6   Were entirely ready to have *Hold My Gold* remove all these defects of character.

7   Humbly asked the authors of *Hold My Gold* to remove our shortcomings.

8 Made a list of all persons affected by our wackness and became willing to make amends to them all.

9 Made direct amends to such people wherever possible, except when to do so would in itself be wack.

10 Continue to take personal inventory and, when wack, promptly admit it.

11 Sought, through smoking blunts and gyrating in bikinis, to improve our chances of possible contact with Lil Jon, praying only for knowledge of His will for us and the power to carry that out.

12 Having had a spiritual awakening as a result of these steps, we tried to carry this message to other wack white girls and practice crunkness in all our affairs. Holla!

Letters from Our Readers

To prove that you are not alone in your white wackness, we have compiled just a few out of the hundreds of letters we receive every day from confused white gals just like you. Here are some FAQs.

Dear HMG,

I am a fellow white girl who, unfortunately, was born sans rhythm. It is very tough for me to attend social gatherings. What am I to do?

Rhythmless in Portland,

Amy

Dear Amy,

When in doubt, or out of rhythm, the answer is always this: Wear fewer clothes.

Dear HMG,

I have moved from Madison, Wisconsin, to Atlanta, Georgia, to facilitate the pursuit of a more hip-hop lifestyle. In moving here, I have found that many of the locals are calling me a "poser." What do I do?

Hurt in Hotlanta,

Kasey

Dear Kasey,
If they start "frontin'," you should "cut 'em." This will surely stop them from further questioning your authenticity.

Dear HMG,

I live a happy, well-rounded life in Greenwich, Connecticut. My parents are together, I have a great group of gal pals, and my trust fund has made law school a real possibility. What truly plagues me is my lack of appreciation for, and understanding of, Jay-Z. I know that he is well-respected in the hip-hop circles I long to frequent. Can you help me?

Clueless in Connecticut,

Molly

Dear Molly,

First of all, what da fuck are you still doing in Greenwich? Secondly, we are glad you decided to ask us about Jay-Z's legitimacy first, simply because if you had asked anybody else, they would have been so infuriated by your ignorance that they may have slashed your face with a box cutter and/or possibly taken your wallet. We too have at one time questioned Jay-Z's magic, but, after various altercations and some stolen credit cards, we have come to understand that, in the hip-hop world, Jay-Z (a.k.a. Hova) is the king. When it comes to this specific issue, it's best that you do not ask questions. Just follow.

Dear HMG,

I was heading back from my afternoon Pilates class, when a man on the street stopped me and complimented me on my "sweet cakes." Now, I'm no baker, and having just exercised, I can positively tell you that I was not carrying any pastries or carbs. What did this gentleman mean?

Cake-free in Colorado,

Katie

Dear Katie,

Thank you for your question. It is very important that we address this issue, as you will hear it often at da club, da mall, and even da store. This gentleman was well aware of the fact that you were not carrying any baked goods. Instead, what he was trying to convey was his appreciation for your physique. "Cakes" is another term for a woman's round, firm buttocks. Smile! People like you!

Dear HMG,

*I have been reading a lot about the "Dirty South."
As an environmentalist, I am concerned about pollution
and littering. Is the South really that dirty and, if so, what
can I do to help?*

Bummed in Berkeley,

Sally

Dear Sally,

Girl, it's the "Derrrrty South" and we like to keep it that way, because, as Bone Crusher so eloquently put it, "Hotlanta be da shit." In addition, being an environmentalist is known in hip-hop circles as being mad, mad, mad wack. Take your mind off Greenpeace, and start concentrating on getting da green. Holla dolla!

AMANDA McCALL & ALBERTINA RIZZO

Da 4-1-1: A Guide to Hold My Gold Sidebars

Da Rulz These sidebars highlight or expand on important rules of hip-hop!

Wuss Wut Here you will find definitions of hip-hop terms!

Did You Know? These sidebars provide cultural and historical facts about hip-hop!

These recurring characters provide notes on dialect, idioms, and vocabulary, and give words of encouragement that may or may not at all pertain to the lesson.

Snoop Sez

Lil' Kim Sez

Lil Jon Sez

Paul E. Pimp's Wordz of Wizdum

Fat Joe

Kingpin Skinny Pimp

Amanda McCall & Albertina Rizzo

Chapter by chapter, *Hold My Gold* will provide you with a well-rounded education in all things crunk. This guide will teach you how to recognize and adopt the key characteristics of a rapper and rap music. You will excel in basic hip-hop subjects such as loose women, violence, gratuitous sex, extremely expensive cars and houses, nightclubs, illicit drugs, alcohol, gold dental work, and exceedingly large and shiny jewelry. By the time you reach the end of this book, you will have earned a Ph.D. in thuggin' and will be ready to journey out of your pasty, rhythmless shell and into the world of hip-hop splendor!

So come aboard this gold-encrusted, tinted-windowed, ho-filled hip-hop train. We are leaving Whiteyville! Next stop, Crunktown! All aboard, bitches! *(Toot! Toot!)*

1 DA BASIX: Vocabulary, Grammar, & Translation

I. Hip-Hoptionary:
Useful Words and Phrases

Following is an abbreviated dictionary of helpful hip-hop terms.

Rip out this section and tuck it into your backpack, purse, or bra.

Bring it with you wherever you go. Remember, repetition is the

key to learning the language of hip-hop. Practice every day and,

before you know it, you will be able to understand and/ or

converse with any rapper! It's that simple!

BENT: Getting intoxicated; inebriated; drunkenness not necessarily relating to but possibly including the act of vomiting due to consumption of alcoholic beverages. Example: "Damn, Jill, dat Napa Valley Chardonnay we snuck into the Tori Amos concert got me crazy bent!"

> Hott Tip!: **Fully immersing yourself in the language of hip-hop is essential if you want to achieve fluency. Aside from constantly listening to hip-hop music, it is also important that you spend time in places frequented by rappers and hip-hop moguls. Going to check out the new Hillary Duff flick? Why not skip it and spend the day standing at the counter of Jacob the Jeweler hovering over customers? Instead of a game of badminton with your friends, spend the afternoon at a Cadillac Escalade dealership!**

CHRONIC: High-quality marijuana. Example: "If you want to be a cool person, smoke the chronic."

DAT ALBUM IS DA KNOCK: A very good compilation or record. Example: "Yo, Bridget, I heard the new Clay Aiken Christmas album! Dat album is da knock!"

DROP-TOP: An automobile with a top that can be folded back or removed. Example: "Last summer on the Vineyard, my gal pals and I spent the afternoons driving around in my drop-top, blasting Matchbox Twenty."

5-0: Law enforcement officials. Example: "Yo, Jenny! 5-0! Let's go say hi!"

FRONT: The act of pretending to be someone or something you are not; disingenuousness. Example: "Muffy, don't even front like you don't like Aaron Carter. I saw his fourth CD, *Another Earthquake,* in your Volvo."

G-UNIT: Popular rap artist 50 Cent's close-knit group of friends, consisting of Tony Yayo (formerly incarcerated), Lloyd Banks, Young Buck, Game and others. Known for their large muscles and interest in semiautomatic weapons. Example: "G-Unit is the most innovative musical trio since Peter, Paul, and Mary."

ICED-OUT: Diamond-encrusted and/or adorned. Example: "Look at the iced-out tennis bracelet Dad got Grandma!"

IT COSTS TA FLOSS: Acknowledging the funds necessary to finance expensive and gaudy merchandise, such as gem-encrusted pimp goblets. Example: "Yo, Katie, I'm deep in debt. But it's no biggie, 'cause it costs ta floss!"

JUS' CUT ME DA CHECK: Asking if it would be possible to receive one's paycheck promptly. Other examples: "I gots to get mine," "Where my money at?," or "Muthafucka, I said pay me!"

MURDA: Often yelled at da club, da store, or da theada'. In the right hip-hop circles, this usually means the person yelling is either a former member of Murda Inc. or that they are having a bloody good time. Example: "That last round of Scattergories sure was fun . . . Murda!"

(*Caution:* If you hear this at a white person's party, dial 911, as chances are that someone is actually being murdered and, therefore, law enforcement agents should be notified immediately.)

PO-PO: See *5–0*. Example: "The sailing regatta after-party got so crunk, I thought for sure someone was gonna call the po-po."

PIMP CUP: Gem-encrusted goblet of crunkness held by playas and/or pimps. Example: "Mother, please stop eating your oatmeal out of my pimp cup!"

SEED: Child (often conceived out of wedlock). Example: "Hold my seed, Kasey. I'm going to the organic market."

STUNT: The act of displaying one's valuables in a manner that may inspire awe or intrigue; to show off. Example: "Lucy be stuntin' with that new J. Crew cashmere cardigan set!"

PAUL E. PIMP'S WORDZ OF WIZDUM: "Words are like weapons, except they ain't made of steel and they don't got bullets in 'em and you can't put 'em in yo' car."

TEARIN' UP DA CLUB: Having a good time. Can also mean that a fight has ensued and the participants are literally tearing the club into pieces, which would result in a bad time. Example of a good time: "Yo, Holly, we were really crunk last night. We were tearing up da club, girl!" Example of a bad time: "Those fellows had beef with each other and started tearing up da club, girl!"

THROWED: See *Bent*. Example: "Yo, Sally, I was really throwed at the bris yesterday. I had, like, two Zimas and a wine cooler."

THUGGIN': Relating to the lifestyle of a gangsta, one that is characterized by shooting guns and drinking champagne in clubs. Example: "Daddy bought a ton of pretty fireworks for our Fourth of July party this year. Our family was straight thuggin'."

II. Grammar

White Root	Hip-Hop Spelling	Pronunciation
The	Da	Duh
Dirty	Derrrty	Duhrrr-tee
Fronting	Frontin'	Fruhn-ehn
Thugging	Thuggin'	Thug-ehn
Balling	Ballin'	Bawl-ehn
Dollar	Dolla'	Dawl-ah
Holler	Holla'	Hawl-ah
Murder	Murda'	Merrr-duh
Player	Playa'	Pley-uh
Theater	Theada'	Thee-ah-duh
Logistics	Logiztix	Low-jiz-ticks

White Root	Hip-Hop Spelling	Pronunciation
Pap Smear	Papsmerrr	Paps-ma-err
Literary	Litrrrray	Luh-Uh-Errrr-Eee
Diarrhea	Derrrrrr	Duh-urrrr-ah
Pneumonia	Pnah Monya	Puh-nuh-mo-knee uuhh

SNOOP SEZ: "Bodizzle, nizzle twizzle, lizzle boo-boobabizzle."

III. Translations

Please choose the correct translation for the following sentences:

---

1 *"Yo, less twiss a la."*

    A. "MAN, DO I LOVE BOCA BURGERS!"

    B. "I'D LIKE A LITTLE LESS FOAM IN MY GRANDE SKIM LATTE."

    C. "IS THAT FROZEN YOGURT FAT-FREE?"

    D. "HEY! LET'S ROLL A MARIJUANA CIGARETTE!"

LIL' KIM SEZ: "Fuck you!"

AMANDA McCALL & ALBERTINA RIZZO

2 *"I wuz cold-lampin' wit a cavy sack in the A-T-L sippin' Oh-E 'n' gettin' bent."*

A. "My interior designer friend suggested I buy some lamps for the foyer."

B. *Caddyshack* is one of my favorite Bill Murray movies."

C. "My yoga class has made me so flexible. Look how far I can bend!"

D. "I was relaxing with a bag of marijuana in Atlanta, Georgia, enjoying a single-serving, forty-ounce bottle of Olde English "800" Malt Liquor, getting rather intoxicated!"

3 *"Homey curried my cuz, 'n' sprayed up my mama's crib, so I done gave dat muthafucka a curb job biatch!"*

A. "The *New York Times* food critic gave it a B, but said that the curried tofu appetizer is to die for!"

B. "I don't usually go for spray tans, but my dermatologist suggested it as an alternative to sunbathing."

C. "I heard Dexatrim really helps to curb your appetite and lessens your cravings for carbs!"

D. "A fellow spoke of my cousin in an unfriendly manner, and then proceeded to open fire on my mother's residence. In retaliation, I attacked that fellow by thrusting his dental cavity onto the cement confine barrier of a road."

4 *"Girl, I got cream comin' out my ass . . . you wanna piece o' dis?"*

    A. "THIS MAY BE A PERSONAL QUESTION, BUT HAVE YOU EVER SUFFERED FROM ANAL LEAKAGE?"

    B. "MY MOM'S KEY LIME PIE IS FABULOUS, WOULD YOU LIKE TO TRY A PIECE?"

    C. "BRIDGET, I JUST FOUND THIS DIVINE ALPHA-HYDROXY CREAM FROM ESTÉE LAUDER AT BLOOMIE'S!"

    D. "HELLO, LADY. I HAVE MONEY, RICHES, AND VALUABLES. WOULD YOU LIKE TO HAVE SEXUAL INTERCOURSE WITH ME?"

ANSWER KEY: All answers are *D,* as in *Da Answer.*

IV. Composition Skillz: Writing Your Own Rap Song

You may think that because rappers get paid so much money, writing a rap song is super hard. But, as you will see in the following activity, composing a rap song is super-duper fun and easy! To create your very own rap verse, simply fill in each blank with one of the words listed below. To make your rap longer, just repeat the first verse using different words from the list. You'll have a record deal in no time.

Loyalty	*Ass*
Larceny	*Gat*
Robbery	*A.K.*
Murda'	*Ice*
Bitch	*Gold*
Booty	*Platinum*
Dick	*Leather Interior*
Deez nuts	*Lexus*
Titty	*Benz*

AMANDA McCALL & ALBERTINA RIZZO

Caddy	*Drank*
Dubs	*Smoke*
Strip clubs	*Pimp*
Jacuzzis	*Ho*
Moët	*Ball*
Cristal	*Thug*
Hennessy	*Fuck*
Chronic	*Smack*
Blunts	*Rub*

_____ and _____ make yo' booty bounce.

_____ -ing in da V.I.P. room or da backseat of ma _____.

Mo' _____, mo' _____, mo' _____, dats how we do.

Drankin' _____, smokin' _____, fuckin' _____, and

bustin' _____, mothafucka.

Chorus: _____ _____ _____ _____ _____ bitch.

_____ _____ _____ _____ _____ ho.

_____ _____ _____ _____ _____ bitch.

_____ _____ _____ _____ _____ ho, fuck you.

V. Chapter Exercises

1 *All of the following are hip-hop pseudonyms for marijuana cigarettes except:*

    A. Sess.

    B. Dope.

    C. Chronic.

    D. Wacky Tabacky.

Amanda McCall & Albertina Rizzo

Complete the following sentences:

---

2 *When a rapper is happy, he says: "Damn, it feels good to be a _____!"*

    A. GOOD PERSON.

    B. FLOWER.

    C. DANCER.

    D. GANGSTA.

---

3 *When a rapper is angry, he says: "I'll pop a _____ in his ass!"*

    A. BUBBLE.

    B. POOP.

    C. CAT.

    D. CAP.

4 *When a rapper is disappointed, he says: "Yo, I spent all my C-notes at da club and it wasn't even_____. I was mad disappointed."*

    A. CHAPERONED.

    B. WELL-CATERED.

    C. FUNNY-HAT NIGHT.

    D. BANGIN'.

AMANDA McCALL & ALBERTINA RIZZO

5 *When a rapper sees an attractive lady, he says: "Shorty's mad fine, she got _____."*

A. HOTT CAKES.

B. DUMPS LIKE A TRUCK.

C. A BUMPIN' BOOTY.

D. BOOTYLICIOUSNESS.

E. JUNK IN DA TRUNK.

F. A STACK IN DA BACK.

G. A GREAT PERSONALITY.

H. ALL EXCEPT *G*.

6 *If you are "blasting" at a party, you are*

    A. SHOWING EVERYONE YOUR NEW CLOGS.

    B. HAVING A BLAST WATCHING *SAY ANYTHING* AND
EATING COOKIE DOUGH WITH YOUR BEST GAL PALS.

    C. PLAYING TWISTER AND GIGGLING.

    D. PLAYING BOISTEROUS MUSIC AND SMOKING CRACK.

7 *If you have "deuce deuces," you*

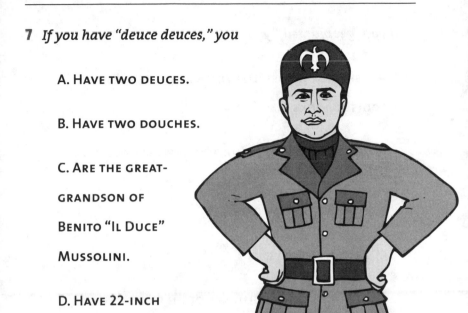

A. Have two deuces.

B. Have two douches.

C. Are the great-grandson of Benito "Il Duce" Mussolini.

D. Have 22-inch rims on the tires of your car.

8 *If you "get blunted," you*

A. ASK YOUR HAIRSTYLIST FOR A BLUNT BOB À LA LOUISE BROOKS.

B. WERE BLUNT WITH YOUR PSYCHOPHARMACOLOGIST WHEN SHE SUGGESTED YOU UP YOUR ANTIDEPRESSANT MEDICATION.

C. GET TOTALLY PSYCHED!

D. ARE UNDER THE INFLUENCE OF AN EXTREMELY LARGE CIGARETTE FILLED WITH DA CHRONIC.

ANSWER KEY: All answers are *D,* as in *Da Answer.*

Bonus Section: Why G Is the Best Letter in the Alphabet

The only letter in the alphabet a true playa' needs to be familiar with is the letter *G*. The next time someone approaches you to argue that *L* or *R* is the best letter, you must tell them that they are frontin'. Just look at all the fabulous words that begin with the letter *G*!

GA-DONK-A-DONK-DONK (as pertaining to your most important body part)

GANG (as pertaining to your best gal pals)

GANGSTA (as pertaining to an inspirational figure in your life)

GANJA (as pertaining to what should be stored in your sock drawer or bra at all times)

GATS (see *Guns*)

G'D UP (as pertaining to what you should be at all times)

GEORGIA (as pertaining to Hotlanta, the Capital of Crunk)

G-FUNK (as pertaining to the era)

GIGANTIC (as pertaining to jewelz)

GIN (as pertaining to what Snoop sips with juice)

GLAMOUR (as pertaining to bikinis and Jacuzzis)

GLOCK (see *Gun* or *Gat)*

GOLD (as pertaining to your desired tooth color)

GRAND LARCENY (as pertaining to a fun hobby)

GRANDMA (as pertaining to she who is the Original Baby Mamma)

 SNOOP SEZ: "Ain't nuthin' but a *G*-thang, baby."

GRENADE (as pertaining to what you throw at bitches who are wack)

GREY GOOSE (as pertaining to getting crunk)

GRINDING (as pertaining to what you should do with strangers in clubs)

G-STRING (as pertaining to what you should wear while grinding with strangers in clubs)

GUARANTEED (as pertaining to whether you will be getting crunk this weekend)

GUCCI (as pertaining to one of the many logos that should adorn every inch of your body)

GULP (as pertaining to what you do with Hennessy)

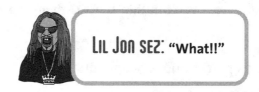

LIL JON SEZ: "What!!"

G-UNIT (as pertaining to a group of creative, insightful, and inspirational young musicians)

GUNS (as pertaining to a cute accessory)

GYRATING (as pertaining to what is done on the hood of a car)

GZA (as pertaining to the cousin of the RZA)

2 HIP-HOP HIZTORY: Vol. 1

In Da Beginning, There Wuz . . .

It is one thing to talk like a pimp, but if you have no knowledge of the history of crunkness, your words have no meaning. Before you can begin to use the hip-hop words and phrases you learned in the previous chapter, you must first stop and take a moment to understand the origins of crunkness and its relationship to wackness.

A Lesson in Ancient Pimpidean Philosophy

Though hip-hop music did not arise until the early 1980s, hip-hop's philosophical foundations date all the way back to Ancient Greece. The philosopher Pimpides was the first to recognize that "the universe can be divided equally into two separate spheres: the Crunkosphere, containing all that is crunk, and the Wackosphere, containing all that is wack"(4870 B.C.). Pimpides became increasingly immersed in his meditations on crunkospherical systems of theory and soon wrote a major treatise disproving the validity of wackness. His groundbreaking hypothesis claimed that crunk activities such as "hangin' with naked bitches" and "wearing excessive jewelry whilst intoxicated" were more beneficial to mankind than wackospherical activities such

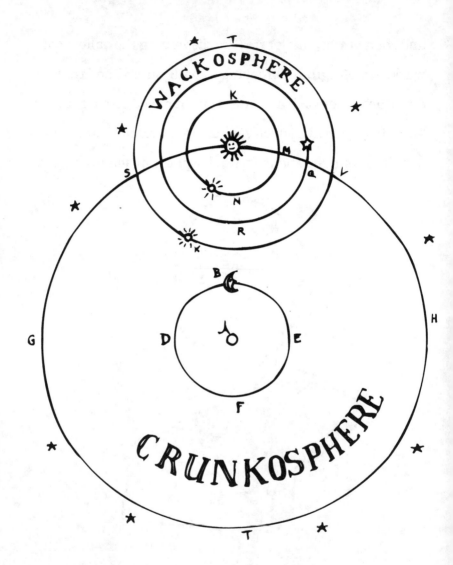

as remaining sober and sacrificing sheep entrails. Pimpides argued that crunkness was, therefore, the basis of civilized society.

Pimpides' philosophy influenced scholars, artists, and writers alike, particularly in the Renaissance, when it was rediscovered and incorporated into the work of masters such as Leonardo, Michelangelo, and Brunelleschi (it's no coincidence that Florence's Il Duomo [Italian for "the titty"] looks like a humungous breast). In his recently discovered secret letters to Bernardo di Escalade, Michelango wrote that "D'ora in poi dipingerò soltanto puttane nude!" (From now on, I will only paint naked bitches!)

Recently, Shakespearean scholars uncovered what they believe to be original drafts of some of William Shakespeare's greatest works, which may have been directly influenced by what came to be known as the Pimpidean (or "Pimp") movement. According to

researchers, these lost plays include titles such as *King Pimp, Titties Andronicus, Taming of the Ho, Much Ado About Bitches, Two Gangstas of Verona, Twelfth Blunt,* and his lost masterpiece, *Macbitch.*

You may be wondering why a basic familiarity with the history of hip-hop is so important for the white gal. How could *you* ever truly understand the socioeconomic implications inherent in its history, one which you may view as existing in an entirely different emotional and geographical context than that with which you are familiar? The roots of hip-hop may be mad phat, but "What," you ask yourself, "do they have to do with me?"

In school, you probably spent much of your time studying the history of Western literature, science, and philosophy. Your knowledge of European history is,

 WUSS WHAT: *Phat* = n. cool; not to be confused with obese . . . which is also cool, but only if you are a rapper.

therefore, probably far greater than that of hip-hop history. Taking that into account, this chapter is meant to expand your knowledge of hip-hop history by relating the major historical playaz in the history of the hip-hop world to major figures in Western history. Soon, you'll learn that the roots of hip-hop have everything to do with you. Let's begin!

	BOLSHEVIKS	PUBLIC ENEMY
Real Name	Bolsheviks	William Drayton, Carlton Douglas Ridenhouer, Richard Griffin, & Norman Lee Rogers
Born	Moscow, Russia, 1917	Los Angeles, CA, 1982
Claim to Fame	Fought the power of the czar	Fought the power of "The Man"
Distinguishing Feature	Angry mob	Camouflage fatigues and onstage military maneuvers
Beef	The czar	The white man
Pioneer of	Bolshevik revolutions!	Wearing clocks as necklaces!

	VINCENT VAN GOGH	2PAC (R.I.P.)
Real Name	Vincent Van Gogh	Tupac Amaru Shakur (R.I.P.)
Born	Groot-Zundert, Netherlands, 1853	Brooklyn, NY, 1971
Claim to Fame	*Starry Night,* tormented life	*If I die 2nite,* "Thug Life" tattoo on his chest
Distinguishing Feature	Chopped-off ear	Ear for phat beats
Beef	Gauguin	Biggie
Pioneer of	Expressionism	Expressin' his thugness

Paul E. Pimp's Wordz of Wizdum:
"Pimpin' ain't e-z, but hiztory iz!"

AMANDA McCALL & ALBERTINA RIZZO

	ALBERT EINSTEIN	**RUN DMC**
Real Name	Albert Einstein	Joseph Simmons, Darryl McDaniels, & Jason Mizell (R.I.P.)
Born	Württemburg, Germany, 1879	Hollis, Queens, NY, 1982
Claim to Fame	Revolutionary Theory of Relativity	Revolutionary theory that Adidas are really, really cool
Distinguishing Feature	Crazy hair	Crazy style
Beef	Nazis	N/A
Pioneer of	20th-century physics	21st-century phatness

	BENEDICT ARNOLD	**VANILLA ICE**
Real Name	Benedict Arnold	Robert Van Winkle
Born	Norwich, CT, 1741	Miami, FL, 1968
Claim to Fame	Turncoat	Turncoat
Distinguishing Feature	American in British army garb	White boy in Hammer pants
Beef	His own cowardice	His own wackness
Pioneer of	Treason	Treason

	HENRY THE VIII	SNOOP DOGG
Real Name	Henry the VIII	Calvin Broadus
Born	Greenwich, England, 1491	Long Beach, CA, 1972
Claim to Fame	Murder and pronounced sexual promiscuity	Alleged murder, and pronounced sexual promiscuity
Distinguishing Feature	Big crown	Big blunt
Beef	Ugly women and the law	Ugly women and the law
Pioneer of	Divorce	Tha hizzle-dizzle fo' shizzle

	NAPOLÉON	**NOTORIOUS B.I.G. (R.I.P.)**
Real Name	Napoléon Bonaparte	Christopher Wallace (R.I.P.)
Born	Corsica, 1769	Brooklyn, NY, 1972
Claim to Fame	Making himself emperor	Making himself big
Distinguishing Feature	Really short	Really big
Beef	Lord Wellington	Tupac
Pioneer of	Napoléon complex	Complex "Baby Mama Drama"

	LOUIS THE XIV	**P. DIDDY**
Real Name	Louis the XIV	Sean Combs
Born	St. Germain-en-laye, France, 1638	Harlem, NY, 1969
Claim to Fame	Sun King	Bling bling
Distinguishing Feature	Phat pad in Versailles	Phat pad in the Hamptons
Beef	Hapsburgs of Austria	Sloppy dressers
Pioneer of	Extravagant parties	Extravagant parties

 LIL JON SEZ: "Okay!"

HIP-HOP HIZTORY: Vol. II . . . Da Saga Continues

(A.K.A. DA RETURN OF DA HIZTORY, A.K.A. STILL HISTORISIZIN')

I. Who Dat?

If you want to run in crunker social circles, you must be familiar with the following abbreviated lists of rappers. To help you remember who's who, we've divided popular rappers into six basic categories that white girls can easily understand: Little, Big, Scary, Friendly, Zany, and Sexy. As with the Hip-Hoptionary, you should rip this out and keep it with you for easy reference at parties, clubs, jewelry stores, and Escalade dealerships to prevent you from feeling left out.

The following is an example of how to use this list:

Situation: You are at a crunk party and someone tells you how much he loves the new Busta Rhymes album.

What to Do: Instead of panicking, simply go to the ladies' room and, while hidden in a stall, find Busta Rhymes on your Who Dat? list. Return to the conversation by exclaiming: "Oh, I too love Busta Rhymes! He sure is ZANY!"

LITTLE: *This category pertains to rappers who were or are still either underweight, underage, or under five feet tall.*

Lil Jon

Lil' Flip

Lil Wayne

Lil' Romeo

Lil' Kim

Lil Scrappy

Too $hort

WUSS WHAT: Jacob the Jeweler = n. one of the greatest men who ever lived; jeweler to the stars; purveyor of your first million-dollar purchase.

BIG: *This category pertains to plus-size rappers who, due to thyroid problems or obsessive compulsive overeating, remained extremely and often obscenely large throughout their careers.*

Fat Joe

Big Pun

Biggie Smalls

Bone Crusher

Heavy D

DID YOU KNOW?: Jesus is responsible for almost every Grammy any rapper ever received!

SCARY: *This category pertains to rappers whom, due to the often frightening subjects they explore in their lyrics (armed robbery, double and/or triple homicide, and international drug cartels), we find slightly intimidating.*

Cash Money Crew (Baby, Mannie Fresh, Juvenile, & friends)

DMX

G-Unit (50 Cent, Young Buck, Lloyd Banks, & friends)

Ghetto Boyz

N.W.A. (Dr. Dre, Eazy-E, Ice Cube, & friends)

Trick Daddy

FRIENDLY: *This category pertains to rappers whose lyrics deal with comforting subjects such as family, love, festivities, food and wine, sneakers, luxury goods, and paychecks.*

Will Smith

Nelly

P. Diddy

Bow Wow

Twista

De La Soul

Run DMC

Kanye West

ZANY: *This category pertains to rappers who often wear silly outfits in their videos and have an affinity for either dancing children, talking animals, or traveling circuses.*

Busta Rhymes

Missy Elliot

Ludacris

Outkast

Snoop

 SNOOP SEZ: "Bitches, I'm zany."

SEXY: *This category pertains to rappers who rap about having sexual intercourse in Jacuzzis, luxury cars, bathrooms, bedrooms, dance floors, and champagne rooms.*

R. Kelly

Cassidy

2 Live Crew

LL Cool J

Pharell Williams

II. Hip-hop Geography: Where You At?

Geography plays a huge part in hip-hop history and, as an American, it is your patriotic duty to understand the states of our fair country according to their hip-hop significance. Do not be overwhelmed. It is only important that you know of certain states, as many have seceded from the Union of Crunk by neglecting to provide any crunkness

whatsoever. They have formed their own Axis of Wackness, and must therefore be disregarded and viewed as enemy states by those who are or long to be crunk.

The following is a list of enemy states:

Alabama	Iowa
Alaska	Kansas
Arizona	Kentucky
Arkansas	Louisiana
Colorado	Maine
Connecticut	Maryland
Delaware	Massachusetts
Hawaii	Minnesota
Idaho	Mississippi
Indiana	Montana

AMANDA McCALL & ALBERTINA RIZZO

Nebraska	Rhode Island
Nevada	South Carolina
New Hampshire	South Dakota
New Jersey	Tennessee
New Mexico	Texas
North Carolina	Utah
North Dakota	Vermont
Ohio	Washington
Oklahoma	West Virginia
Oregon	Wisconsin
Pennsylvania	Wyoming

 DA RULZ: All 134,000 citizens of Sioux Falls, South Dakota, are wack.

III. Know Your Crunkography: Crunk Density Map

 Did You Know?: Slovenia, Uruguay, East Timor, and parts of northern Finland don't even have video hoes.

IV. Crunkographical Awards

The following states receive honorable recognition for contributing to the crunkness of America.

Best place to get crunk and naked and see lots of money: Las Vegas, Nevada

Most Gangsta State: Texas (Highest number of state executions per year: "Texas, you CRAZY!")

Best Come-Back State: Florida

Lifetime Achievement Award: Georgia

Most Crunkness per Capita: New York

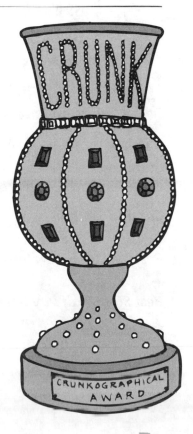

Best New State to Join Union of Crunk: Missouri

Best Duo: North and South Carolina

 WUSS WUT: Da 213 = (duh-too-won-threy) n. gangsta's paradise; sacred birthplace of Warren G., Dr. Dre, and Eazy-E; area code for Compton

Best Work as an Ensemble:
Mississippi, Alabama, Tennessee

Crunkest State to Overcome the Fact That It Borders Canada: Michigan

Best Lil' State: New Jersey

Best State Halfway Between New York and Hotlanta: Virginia

State with First Pimp President: Arkansas

V. Beef 101: Beefin' fo' Beginnaz

Much has changed throughout the history of hip-hop, but one thing has remained the same, and that is the importance of having "beef." Jay-Z had it with Nas, 50 Cent had it with Ja Rule, Los Angeles had it with New York, and now you can have it too!

 Wuss Wutt: "Beef" n. Drinking too much Haterade and having the overwhelming urge to pop a cap in someone's ass.

Hott Tip!: Starting beef with someone is one of the quickest and easiest ways to gain respect in the hip-hop world. Most rappers tend to start beef with other rappers, but, for the white girl, this is not recommended. Instead of starting beef with Dr. Dre or Roc-A-Fella Records, we suggest you start beef with safer, less threatening people and/or objects, such as your grandmother or seafood. Don't like the effects of tryptophan? Why not start beef with turkey? Sick of Mounties? Start beefin' with Canada! The following are people and things we recommend for easy beefin': infants, furniture, germs, canned goods, Girl Scouts, nuns and clergymen, ribbons, Belgium, and embryonic reptiles.

AMANDA McCALL & ALBERTINA RIZZO

VI. Chapter Exercises

1 *Connect da Beef:*

JA RULE	TUPAC
BIGGIE	NAS
JAY-Z	50 CENT
SUGE KNIGHT	BEENIE MAN
IRV GOTTI	VANILLA ICE
BOUNTY KILLAH	DR. DRE

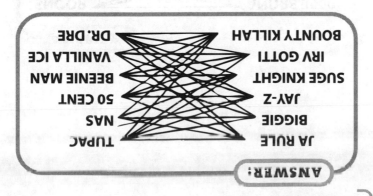

ANSWER!

2 *Connect da Cuz*

SNOOP   ANDRE 3000

BIG BOI   WARREN G

RZA   GZA

DR. DRE   NATE DOGG

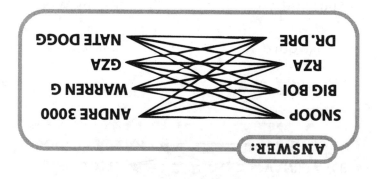

ANSWER:

SNOOP
BIG BOI
WARREN G
ANDRE 3000
NATE DOGG
GZA
RZA
DR. DRE

AMANDA McCALL & ALBERTINA RIZZO

3 *All of the following rappers have at one time been members of the Wu Tang Clan except:*

A. Raekwon

B. Rakeem

C. RZA

D. GZA

E. Ghostface Killah

F. Ol' Dirty Bastard

G. Method Man

H. U-God

I. Masta Killa

J. Inspectah Deck

K. 60 Second Assassin

L. Power Cipher

M. Wise the Civilized

N. Cappadonna

O. Big Baby Jesus

P. Dirt McGirt

Q. None of the above

4 *What unit of measurement is predominantly used in the Union of Crunk?*

    A. HECTACRES

    B. METERS

    C. ACRES

    D. G-G-G-G G-UNIT!

---

5 *Using numbers 1 to 4 (4 being the least), please place the following people in order according to whom you would least like to have beef with:*

    A. SADDAM HUSSEIN

    B. SHANNON DOHERTY

    C. 50 CENT

    D. BOW WOW (WHEN HE WAS STILL LIL')

6 *Not A.K.A.* The following rappers are known by many names and it is important to be familiar with them all. In the following exercises, please identify which A.K.A. the rapper in question has never been known as:

I. Puff Daddy:

A. P. DIDDY

B. DIDDY

C. SEAN COMBS

D. PUFF DADDY

E. PUFFY

F. PUFF

G. PUFFY PUFF

II. Snoop:

A. Snoop Dogg

D. Calvin Broadus

B. Snoop Doggy Dogg

E. Tha Doggfatha

C. Cordazar Broadus

F. Snoopy

 Snoop Sez: "Whut's ma muthafuckin' name?"

III. Outkast's Big Boi and Andre:

A. Daddy Fatsacks and Andre 3000

C. Billy Ocean and Nookie Blossumgang

B. Lucious Leftfoot and Possum Allauishis Jenkins

D. Strawberry Shortcake and the Nasty Purple Pie-Man

IV. Notorious B.I.G.:

A. CHRISTOPHER WALLACE

B. BIG POPPA

C. BIGGIE SMALLS

D. BIGGIE

E. BIG

F. 2BIG4U

LIL' KIM SEZ: "Fuck you!"

3 YO' CRIB: A Home for the Homeys

Now that you've learned who all the rappers are,

it's time to get ready to invite them over to your house. Your home should *not* be a place for relaxation and contemplation. Instead, sleeping at your house should be like sleeping at da club, a place where the only thing you contemplate is how many bottles of Courvoisier you drank at last night's party. This chapter is designed to help you transform a dismal dwelling into a pimp palace in just a few easy steps.

So pull up your hair in a scrunchy and get ready to work, work on getting crazy bent . . . bitches!

I. Crunkin' Up Yo' Crib:

It is very important that before you start the process of pimpin' up your pad, you get rid of everything remotely white, because, as you may remember from Chapter 1, Whiteness = Wackness. Start by removing all Laura Ashley duvet covers and all decorative tapestries, as they are blatant signs of wackness. Remember, the living room is about living, and you're livin' large! Nothing enlarges a room like having no furniture! Remove all college futons and IKEA coffee tables to make room for your drankin' patnaz and your new entertainment station, which *must* include the following:

- The largest, most expensive sound system you can find
- The largest, most expensive DVD/VCR you can find

- Several of the largest, most expensive flat-screen TVs you can find

- PlayStation 2 and/or Xbox

II. Sample Floor Plan

($) **Rapper**   ⊘ **Stripper pole**   **T.V.**

III. Yo' Nutrition

1. THE HIP-HOP FOOD PYRAMID

It takes a lot of energy to be a gangsta, so, after money, cars, gold, gats, bikinis, diamonds, and Jacuzzis, your health should be your eighth-most important priority. Begin your new health regime by removing all fat-free, low-carb, and/or lo-cal items from your home. Replace with crazy liquor. Be sure your liquor cabinet *always* contains the following items:

Cristal (100 bottles),

Moët (95 bottles),

Hennessy (58 bottles),

Courvoisier (54 bottles),

Chivas Regal (54 bottles),

Tanqueray (50 bottles),

Alizé (50 bottles),

Cognac (30 bottles),

Olde English "800" (100 forty oz. bottles), Colt 45 (115 forty oz. bottles) (put aside 20 bottles for brunches and picnics).

The following food pyramid will rid your body of white-amins and help you stay crunker longer.

AMANDA McCALL & ALBERTINA RIZZO

2. IN THE KITCHEN WITH FAT JOE: COOKIN' WIT CRISTAL

No one knows crunk cooking better than rap superstar Fat Joe. Here, Fat Joe shares some of his favorite classic hip-hop recipes, phat eats guaranteed to turn a drab dinner party into a crunk hip-hop feast!

THE NOTORIOUS P.I.G.

Ingredients:

- A big-ass ham

- A bottle of Cristal

Preparation:

1   Soak da big-ass ham in Cristal for three hours.

2   Throw dat shit in a pan.

3   Crunk up da oven to 450°.

4   Cook dat shit.

The Notorious P.I.G.
featuring Salt & Peppa'

Ingredients:

- -A big-ass ham

- -Salt

- -Peppa'

- -A bottle of Cristal

Preparation:

1　Soak dat big-ass ham in Cristal for three hours.

2　Throw dat shit in a pan.

3　Crunk up da oven to 450°.

4　Cook dat shit.

5　Add salt-n-peppa' to taste.

Snoop sez: "Cognac is the drink that's drank by Gs."

AMANDA McCALL & ALBERTINA RIZZO

CHRONIC EMINEM BROWNIES

Ingredients:

- Eggs
- Suga'
- Flour
- Butta'

- M&Ms
- Cristal
- Da chronic

Preparation:

1. In a big-ass bowl, combine flour, suga', eggs, butta', M&Ms, 1 bottle of Cristal, and an ounce of da chronic.

2. Mix 'til dat shit is mad smooth and creamy.

3. Crunk up da oven 'n' cook dat shit.

4. Get ready to be mad crunk.

Penne à la Pimp

Ingredients:

- Penne pasta
- Tomato sauce
- Cristal

Lil Jon Sez: "Yum!"

Preparation:

1   Cook up da penne.

2   Combine 4 cups tomato sauce 'n' 10 cups Cristal 'n' heat dat shit up.

3   Add pimp sauce to penne and get crunk.

Dusta Limes (a.k.a. Playaz Pie)

Ingredients:

- Mad limes

- Mad Cristal

- Heavy whippin' cream

- Ready-made piecrust

Preparation:

1 Mix mad lime juice wit mad Cristal.

2 Add dat shit to the cream.

3 Whip dat shit up.

4 Pour mixture into ready-made piecrust.

5 Refrigerate for an hour.

6 Sprinkle some pureed chronic for flare.

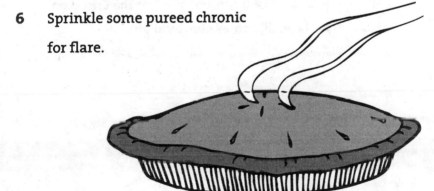

3. FAT JOE'S HOUSEHOLD TIPS:

PROBLEM: *You spill pimp sauce on your brand-new Rocawear tube top.*

 FAT JOE SEZ: Soak dat shit in Cristal.

PROBLEM: *A toddler appears on your doorstep and seems to be choking on a mothball.*

 FAT JOE SEZ: Hold back da lil' seed's head and pour at least a cup and a half of tha Cristal on his face. Lil' homey gon' be aiight.

PROBLEM: *You spent last weekend camping on the Cape and contracted a bad case of poison ivy.*

FAT JOE SEZ: Fill da tub up wit Cristal an' git in thurr. Soak ova' night.

PROBLEM: *Your hamster was just diagnosed with a terminal disease.*

FAT JOE SEZ: Replace his water bottle wit Cristal. If lil' homey gonna go, he gonna go out crunk!

4. HO FOR THE HOLIDAYS: HO, HO, HO-ING WIT LIL' KIM

As you will hear in her yet-to-be released Christmas album, *Santa, Eat My *#!?**, nobody knows holiday cheer better than Lil' Kim. Here she shares a secret recipe that guarantees ho-liday fun for the whole family!

LIL' KIM'S FAMOUS HO-LIDAY WHORE D'OEUVRES (A.K.A. "HO BALLS")

Ingredients:

Lil' butter

Lil' flour

Lil' eggs

Lil' sugar

Several thongs

Lil' Preparation:

1. Preheat oven to 350 degrees.

2. Mix butter, flour, eggs, and sugar until smooth.

3. Scoop out a tablespoon of the mixture and roll it into a lil' ball.

4. Wrap ball in thong and place on buttered cookie sheet. (Make sure to use only silk or lace thong. Polyester and spandex do not breathe and will prevent ho-balls from rising.)

5. Cook for 15 minutes or until thongs begin to brown.

6. Cool for 30 minutes and serve.*

*Remember to unwrap ho-balls before serving. Most thongs are not edible.

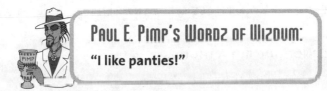

PAUL E. PIMP'S WORDZ OF WIZDUM:
"I like panties!"

Chapter Exercises

1 *Which of the following belongs in your bedroom?*

    A. AN ANTIQUE FLORAL PIN-TUCKED BEDSKIRT.

    B. A WICKER ROCKING CHAIR.

    C. LAND'S END FLANNEL SHEETS.

    D. A RAPPER.

2 *When lounging in your crib, you should be wearing:*

    A. A SOMERSET CARDIGAN WITH ALPINE-INSPIRED PATTERNS.

    B. A MERINO WOOL TWINSET.

    C. AN L.L. BEAN FLEECE MOCK TURTLENECK.

    D. NOTHING BUT A THONG.

AMANDA McCALL & ALBERTINA RIZZO

3 *When throwing a cocktail party, you should serve:*

    A. NORTH ATLANTIC SALMON PATÉ.

    B. CUCUMBER FINGER SANDWICHES.

    C. CARR'S WATER CRACKERS WITH GRUYERE.

    D. FORTIES.

---

4 *On your front lawn, you should have:*

    A. A BIRDFEEDER.

    B. A RECLINING
    ADIRONDACK CHAIR.

    C. A MOSS-GREEN ALL-
    WEATHER GARDEN BENCH.

    D. PIT BULLS.

5 *You are throwing a Fourth of July potluck dinner party. You should ask your guests to bring:*

    A. SPARKLERS.

    B. MAC & CHEESE.

    C. POTATO SALAD.

    D. MAD POT.

6 *Where's the best place to put a Jacuzzi?*

    A. YOUR LIVING ROOM.

    B. YOUR ROOF.

    C. YOUR ESCALADE.

D. Your dining room.

E. Your study.

F. All of the above.

> **ANSWER KEY:** All answers are *D,* as in *Da Answer.*

Lil' Kim Sez: "Fuck you!"

Bonus Section

Yo' Family: Familial Conflict Resolution

For many of you, living with parents and loved ones who neither understand nor fully support your new gangsta lifestyle can make you feel like a stranger in your own home, and, more importantly, prevent you from keepin' it real. The following are some suggestions for dealing with common family conflicts.

Amanda McCall & Albertina Rizzo

CONFLICT: *Your mother asks you if you are remembering to take your women's One-A-Day multivitamins.*

SUGGESTED RESPONSES:

    1. "MOM, I DON'T TAKE VITAMINS. THEY ARE WACK!"

    2. "IF YOU ASK ME AGAIN ABOUT THE VITAMINS, YOU ARE GOING TO GET CUT."

    3. "BITCH, QUIT CALLING ME!"

LIL JON SEZ: "What!"

CONFLICT: *You're in the car with your family for two hours and you suddenly discover that the only available CDs are James Taylor, Joan Baez, and Barbra Streisand's Greatest Hits.*

SUGGESTED RESPONSES:

1. "IF YOU'RE GOING TO PLAY DAT SHIT, I'M GOING TO SIT IN THE TRUNK."

2. "MOM, DAD, YOU POP IN STREISAND, I POP A CAP IN BOTH YOUR ASSES."

3. "BITCHES, STOP THE CAR, MY ASS IS GETTING OUT. I'D RATHER WALK THAN EXPOSE MYSELF TO SUCH UNBEARABLE WACKNESS."

CONFLICT: *Your Aunt Marie sends you a selection of small duck- and teddy-bear-shaped decorative hand soaps from Crabtree & Evelyn for your birthday.*

SUGGESTED RESPONSES:

1. "THANKS, AUNT MARIE, I'D USE THESE SOAPS A LOT! IF I WAS THE WACKEST MOTHERFUCKER IN THE WORLD."

2. "THOSE LITTLE SOAP HOMIES WERE SO WACK, I LINED THEM UP AND SHOT THEM."

3. "BITCH, IF IT ISN'T GOLD, DON'T SEND IT!"

CONFLICT: *Your mother makes tofu meatloaf for dinner.*

SUGGESTED RESPONSES:

1. "MAMA, THAT FOOD BEST BE FOR THE DOG."

2. GRAB THE TOFU MEATLOAF OFF YOUR PLATE AND HURL IT AGAINST THE WALL WHILST YELLING "FUCK TOFU MEATLOAF!"

3. SHOOT THE TOFU MEATLOAF.

CONFLICT: *Your cousin Krissie invites you to her debutante ball in Greenwich.*

SUGGESTED RESPONSES:

1. "THE ONLY BALLS I KNOW BELONG TO BALLAZ, BIATCH!"

2. "THE ONLY THING COMING OUT AT THIS DEBUTANTE BALL IS MY GAT."

3. "YEAH, I'D LOVE TO GO TO YOUR BALL. IF I WAS A CRACKHEAD!"

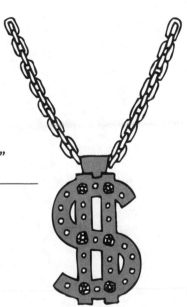

HOLD MY GOLD] 117

4 YO' RIDE: Automotive Advice

The only thing more important than having a crunk

house is having a crunk car. There is no excuse for vehicular wackness. In Crunkville, having a wack ride is a federal offense. DMV records indicate that over 98.4 percent of all white girls own or operate dangerously wack vehicles. The following steps are meant to help you crunk up yo' ride and prevent you from becoming just another statistic.

1. De-Wackin'

- Peel off any Phish, Greenpeace, or PETA stickers.

- Remove any decals and/or other evidence that you attended a small New England liberal arts college.

- Remove any ski and/or bicycle racks.

- Remove your stash of Balance Bars from the backseat.

GRAMMY

- If you drive a Saab or Volkswagon, simply pry off the hood ornament and replace with a more acceptable symbol (i.e., a Benz star, a Jaguar, or, if you can find one, a Grammy).

II. Re-Crunkin'

- Install a top-of-the-line, phat-ass sound system (please include: boomers and tweeters).

- Add TV/DVD/PlayStation 2.

> **Hott Tip!** If you can't afford to bulletproof your ride, just smother it with Crisco. The bullets will slide right off!

● Tint your windows.

● Add hydraulics and drop-tops for true O-G Flava.

> **Hott Tip!**: If you can't fit a Jacuzzi in the back of your ride, try removing all the seats and the steering wheel to create extra space!

● Customize your plates. You may frame them with either neon lights or chains.

● Add rims, preferably dub-spinners to keep in constant floss.

● Include Oakland Raiders and/or any favorite sports team interior (remember: tennis and hockey are not applicable).

III. Cust-O-Mizin'

In the hip-hop world, it's not about what you have, it's about what you have that the other guy doesn't have. When it comes to vehicular phatness, it's quantity, not quality. However, if your budget doesn't allow you to install four plasma TVs up in yo' ride, why not install four copy machines? Remember, it doesn't matter what it is, as long as it's custom-made. Installing several of the following items will transform your generic automobile into a customized crunkmobile and help you put the *O* back in O.G.!

○▷ Replace the passenger-side airbag with a phat sewing machine!

○▷ Take out the engine and install a frozen yogurt dispenser (yumm!).

> **Hott Tip!**: Though Louis Vuitton, Gucci, and Fendi interiors may be all the rage, pricey couture labels are not the only way to achieve automotive floss. Wallpaper and wicker are cute alternatives that will add personal

○▷ Instead of silly TVs, how about pencil sharpeners installed in all four headrests. Now all your homies can do the *New York Times* crossword puzzles in the car!

AMANDA McCALL & ALBERTINA RIZZO

Install an abacus on your dashboard for road trips to count how many Punch Buggies you and your gal pals can spot!

WUSS WUT: Dubs = (duh-bz) n. car accessory; car jewelry; requisite for automotive floss.

Can't afford a bumpin' stereo system in your trunk? Why not a model railroad!

No hydraulics? No problem! Replace the driver's seat with a mini trampoline! You'll be bouncing like you were in a souped-up drop-top. No one will even know the difference!

IV. YO' RIMS

If you are going to floss properly, rims are a must. Some hip-hop experts might even argue that having rims is more important than having a car. In fact, rims are such a symbol of crunkness that it would be a pity not to use them in every facet of your life. The following are some examples of how rims can transform everyday objects into everyday objects with rims!

U. Yo' Plates

Your ride will never be a true thugmobile without customized plates, but choosing a flossin' phrase is a difficult task. The following are some examples of what you should and should not put on your license plate:

Crunk Plates	*Bunk Plates*
OZ	CRAB E
KUTU	WASP E
PA ME	N EMA
2THUGZ4U	I LUV IOS
STR8 G	I PP
RAP R	Q8 WH8

VI. Chapter Exercises

1 *Which of the following is an acceptable color to tint the windows of yo' ride?*

    A. Periwinkle.

    B. Nantucket red.

    C. Taupe.

    D. Gold.

---

2 *What two things do you most look for in a car?*

    A. Safety and reliability.

    B. Comfort and roominess.

    C. Easy handling and gas mileage.

    D. Gold dub spinners and tinted windows.

3 NAME DAT SIGN: *On the road to crunkness, one of the most important skills to develop is the ability to interpret signs. In the following exercise, please identify the meaning of the road signs pictured below.*

1 "No Unloaded Guns"

2 "No Cats with Books"

3 "No Hoes in Clothes"

4 "No Closed Containers"

5 "Caution: Rapper on Ecstasy"

6 "Slow fo' Hoes"

7 "No Fake Jewelz"

8 "Stop Being Wack"

9 "Caution: Bitches in Thongs"

Lil Jon Sez: "Okay!"

Amanda McCall & Albertina Rizzo

5 HOT IN HERRRE: Love Tips

Thugs Are from Mars, Bitches Are from Venus

Having a crunk crib and a crunk ride means nothing if you have no one to share them with. Even the crunkest thugs needs a little romance. In his heartfelt reflection on the human condition, 50 Cent sings that he is "into havin' sex, [he] ain't into makin' love." This sentiment is not only touching, but also extremely instructive. This chapter will shed light on the complexities of being someone's ho, and help guide you in your exploration of love, thug style.

Lil Jon Sez: "What!"

I. WHAT NOT TO SAY ON DATES WITH A RAPPER

▷ I was a Women's Studies major. What did you major in?

▷ Did you know Dave Matthews went solo?

▷ What am I looking for in a guy? Does Tom Hanks in *You've Got Mail* ring a bell?

▷ Isn't Cape Cod fabulous in the summer?

▷ I think my toosh is too big, do you think I should cut back on the carbs?

▷ How 'bout them Rangers?

II. NAME DAT GAT

Knowing what kind of firearm your favorite rapper prefers is as important as remembering your own birthday. The exercise below is designed to test your knowledge of both legal and illegal weapons. Working from the following list, please match the name of the gat with its corresponding image.

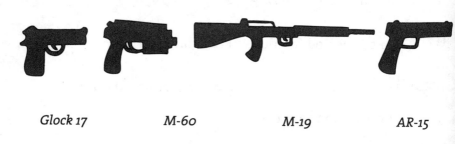

Glock 17   *M-60*   *M-19*   *AR-15*

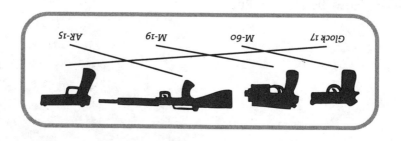

AR-15   M-19   M-60   Glock 17

III. NAME DAT HO: KNOWING YOUR COMPETITION

There are many different types of women in hip-hop, so distinguishing one kind of bitch from another can be a complicated process. This section will help you learn to easily identify hip-hop females by breaking them down into five distinct archetypes.

BABY MAMA

⟡ **DEFINITION:** Mother of homey's baby, but not legally bound to or dating homey.

⟡ **IDENTIFYING FEATURE:** Usually carrying and/or discussing a baby. Often surrounded by lawyers and/or angry family members.

⟡ **HABITAT:** Her own mother's residence.

⟡ **BEHAVIOR:** Usually very angry and tired. Approach with caution.

WIFEY

✧ **DEFINITION:** Legal wife of homey.

✧ **IDENTIFYING FEATURES:** Copious amounts of bling, specifically a wedding ring.

✧ **HABITAT:** Homey's residence.

✧ **BEHAVIOR:** Usually passive but extremely protective over her legal husband.

✧ **NOTE:** Do not confuse wifey with baby mama. Though wifey may have a seed, she is not, by definition, a baby mama.

SHORTY

- ✧ **DEFINITION:** Attractive young woman with whom homey either has sexual intercourse or with whom homey would like to have sexual intercourse.

- ✧ **IDENTIFYING FEATURES:** Tight and minimal clothing. Often surrounded by girlfriends or dancing provocatively with other homies who would like to have sex with her.

- ✧ **HABITAT:** Da club.

- ✧ **BEHAVIOR:** Generally approachable unless provoked, in which case, she will cut ya.

VIDEO HO

◇ **DEFINITION:** Woman in a hip-hop video.

◇ **IDENTIFYING FEATURES:** Few or no clothes. Body usually soaked in water, oil, champagne, or a combination of all three. Always gyrating.

◇ **HABITAT:** Usually in da club, in a bed, in or on a car, by or in a Jacuzzi, next to, under, or on top of a rapper. Straddling a pole.

◇ **BEHAVIOR:** Friendly in front of the camera. May become violent if provoked.

CRACK HO

✧ **DEFINITION:** A promiscuous female who has sexual relations with numerous men in her hood, even ugly mugs, in return for crack.

✧ **IDENTIFYING FEATURES:** Few teeth, skinny, dirty, unkempt. Often carrying a crack pipe.

✧ **HABITAT:** Da crack house.

✧ **BEHAVIOR:** Fairly delirious but still approach with caution.

 WUSS WUT: "Remember: Life ain't nothin' but bitches and money!"

IV. PERSONALITY QUIZ: WHAT TYPE OF HO ARE YOU?

Which of the following items would you prefer to put in your mouth?

> A. GOLD.
>
> B. CRISTAL.
>
> C. A POPSICLE.
>
> D. A CRACK PIPE.

Which of the following would you sell your VCR for?

> A. A HUNDRED DOLLARS.
>
> B. A STROLLER.
>
> C. A NEW TUBE TOP.
>
> D. A VILE OF CRACK.

AMANDA McCALL & ALBERTINA RIZZO

What do you prefer to sleep in?

    A. TWO-THOUSAND-THREAD-COUNT EGYPTIAN
COTTON SHEETS.

    B. A JACUZZI.

    C. A RAPPER'S LAP.

    D. A CRACK HOUSE.

A great way for someone to show you they love you is to

    A. GET YOU PREGNANT.

    B. GIVE YOU MONEY.

    C. POUR CHAMPAGNE ON YOUR CHEST.

    D. GIVE YOU CRACK.

If you could be an animal, you would be a

    A. VERY WEALTHY POODLE.

    B. VERY SEXY CAT.

    C. CRISTAL-SOAKED BUNNY.

    D. CRACK-RIDDEN FERRET.

Which adjective best describes your body?

    A. PREGNANT.

    B. BLING-LADEN.

    C. GREEZY.

    D. CRACK-ADDICTED.

AMANDA McCALL & ALBERTINA RIZZO

When are you most likely to have sex?

    A. WHEN YOU MEET A RAPPER AT AN AFTER-PARTY.

    B. WHEN YOU MEET A RAPPER AT DA CLUB.

    C. WHEN YOU MEET A RAPPER ON DA STREET.

    D. ALL OF THE ABOVE.

ANSWER KEY

IF YOU ANSWERED MOSTLY *A*, CONGRATULATIONS . . .
YOU'RE ABOUT TO BE A BABY MAMA!

IF YOU ANSWERED MOSTLY *B*, BURN THAT PRE-NUP . . .
YOU'RE A WIFEY!

IF YOU ANSWERED MOSTLY *C*, REMOVE YOUR BIKINI TOP AND
LUBE UP . . . YOU'RE A VIDEO HO!

IF YOU ANSWERED MOSTLY *D*, SADLY, WE CANNOT HELP YOU . . .
YOU ARE A CRACK HO.

U. KINGPIN SKINNY PIMP'S WHORE-O-SCOPES: SIGNS OF DA HO-DIAC

AQUARIUS: You are a ho who likes to be sprayed with water when you naked. You are good at sittin' in Jacuzzis.

PISCES: Dis mean you mad smooth, like a fish o' somethin'. You like da beach but also thrive in stretched Navigataz wit Jacuzzis in da back.

ARIES: Dis mean you bounce up 'n' down in da air when you in a video.

TAURUS: You real stubborn about what rappers can pour on yo' chest. Girl, you should jus' relax.

GEMINI: Dis mean you a two-sided ho: Sometimes you a crazy-ass ho, 'n' sometimes you crazy sensitive about havin' yo' ass fondled.

CANCER: Dis mean yo' can is a good dancer. Bitch, shake dat ass!

LEO: Dis is da sign of da tiger, which mean you look real nice in leopard-print bikinis.

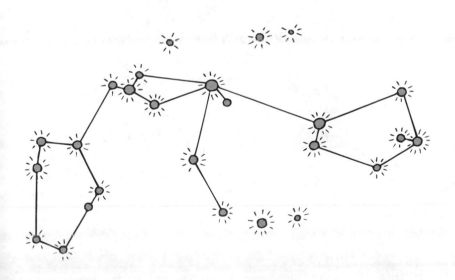

VIRGO: Dis mean you a ho from Virginia.

LIBRA: You a real well-balanced ho: You can balance on da hood of a Bentley while straddling a pole and taking off yo' bikini top.

SCORPIO: Dis mean dat you relate to scorpions because they sting bitches who front.

SAGITTARIUS: You look aiight but you kinda saggy.

CAPRICORN: Dis mean you like to bust caps.

LIL JON SEZ: "What!"

Chapter Exercises

1 *When a rapper visits your crib, the first thing you show him is*

    A. Your antique Limoges Egg collection.

    B. Your new cross-country skis.

    C. The wind chimes you bought this summer in Maine.

    D. Your breasts.

Snoop Sez: "I don't love you, ho, I'm out the do'."

2 *On your first date with a rapper, you suggest*

A. A KAYAKING TRIP.

B. A MATINEE SHOWING OF THE BROADWAY HIT *THOROUGHLY MODERN MILLIE*.

C. A COUPLES' POTTERY CLASS.

D. DOING IT ON THE HOOD OF HIS CADILLAC ESCALADE.

3 *Which of the following is a great date movie?*

A. *THE MIRROR HAS TWO FACES*.

B. *WHITE OLEANDER*.

C. *RUNAWAY BRIDE*.

D. *SNOOP DOGG'S GIRLS GONE WILD: DOGGYSTYLE*.

4 *The morning after you have made love to a rapper, you should*

    A. GO TO BRUNCH AND DISCUSS YOUR FEELINGS OVER PIPING HOT BOWLS OF CINNAMON-RAISIN OATMEAL.

    B. ASK HIM WHERE THE RELATIONSHIP IS GOING AND IF YOU CAN MEET HIS PARENTS.

    C. CUDDLE.

    D. AS HE'S LEAVING, ASK IF YOU CAN BE IN HIS NEXT VIDEO.

ANSWER KEY All answers are *D*, as in *Da Answer*.

6 MAD ICE & CRAZY SKINZ: Clothing & Accessories

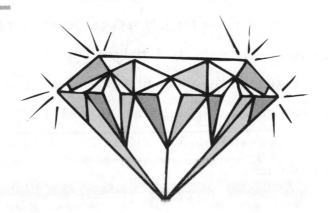

Romance is an important part of the gangsta lifestyle, but without the proper clothing and accessories, any romantic relationship is simply an impossibility. The following chapter will help you perfect your new hip-hop style.

I. BeDazzling Yo' Life

Though it may seem shocking and sad, there are many people in the world who are not familiar with what many consider to be one of the greatest inventions of the twentieth century: The BeDazzler, a standard rhinestone-setting machine on sale for only $14.95 at your local craft store. With the BeDazzler, gold stud appliqué decoration is now as easy as reloading your gun! In fact, throughout this section, imagine the BeDazzler as a gat, but instead of shooting bullets and causing mayhem, it shoots bling and causes crunkness.

SUPER FUN BEDAZZLING PROJEX

1   **ON YOUR CLOTHES:** Lil' Kim, Trina, and Gangsta
    Boo, the most subtle and elegant ladies in hip-hop,
    have proven that there is no such thing as putting too
    many rhinestones on your clothes. Every inch of
    fabric on your body should be gem-encrusted.*

* *REMEMBER:* You should never have more than two to three inches of
fabric on your body.

2   **ON YOUR BODY:** Heading out for a night on the town and can't find a shirt to wear? Just BeDazzle your torso!*

* When BeDazzling your flesh, make sure to have a bottle of hydrogen peroxide and some Q-Tips handy at all times, as infection is likely.

> **Hott Tip!:** If you find yourself walking alongside of the highway late at night, heavily BeDazzled clothing can also serve as a safety device!

AMANDA McCALL & ALBERTINA RIZZO

3 DA BATHROOM: Tranform your toilet from a human waste receptacle into an iced-out throne!*

* Careful when sitting on a BeDazzled toilet seat, as rhinestones are quite sharp and can tear the tender flesh of the buttocks!

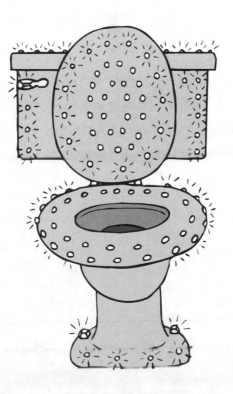

4 DA KITCHEN: With one touch of the BeDazzler, every glass and coffee mug in your kitchen can be transformed into an iced-out pimp cup.*

* Though it may seem like a great idea, try not to BeDazzle your food. BeDazzler brand rhinestones can be difficult to digest and can get trapped in your small intestines.

DID YOU KNOW?: Having lots of cars, clothes, and money will guarantee happiness!

LIL' KIM'S DO-IT-YO'-MUTHAFUCKIN'-SELF BIKINI:

What you'll need:

- bottle caps

- string

- double-sided tape (optional)

Instructions:

LIL' KIM SEZ: "Fuck you!"

II. Business 101: Yo' Empire

In the hip-hop world, you are nothing unless you have your own line of clothes, and, as Baby Phat, Sean John, Rocawear, Fetish, Wu-Wear, P. Miller, G-Unit, and Vokal have shown, starting your own clothing line is as easy as pie.

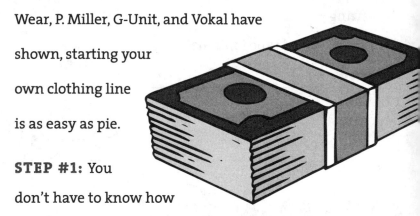

STEP #1: You don't have to know how to rap to have a clothing line, but it *does* help if you have a rapper-like name. The following is a list of name combinations to facilitate your venture into fashion.

The equation is quite simple. Just take a word from Column A and add a word from Column B. Then, finish off your name with Column C!

Note: The less sense your name makes, the crunker it is!

Column A	Column B	Column C
LIL'	DERRTY	LESBIAN
BIG	ADOPTED	PLEBEIAN
OL'	BIPOLA'	MOLESTA'
FAT	DRUNK	BASTARD
PHAT	SOBA'	PREACHA'
YOUNG	UGLY	ACUPUNCTURIST
SOFT	NICE LOOKIN'	PUNISHA'
HARD	PUNCTUAL	CHIROPRACTA'
HOT	STUPID	CRUSHA'
COLD	EMOTIONAL	THUMPA'

Column A	Column B	Column C
SHORT	INAPPROPRIATE	SUCKA'
TALL	SPECIAL	HATA'
PO'	ASIAN	LOVA'
RICH	BAPTIZED	CRAPA'
BALD	CIRCUMSIZED	MASTA'
KIND	ANGRY	PIMPA'
CRUEL	SAD	RAPPA'
FUN	SMELLY	VALEDICTORIAN
DULL	CRAMPY	VETERAN
GAY	LUTHERAN	PODIATRIST
WISE	DOPEY	HO

Column A	Column B	Column C
DUMB	SLEEPY	BITCH
MUTE	SCOOBY	TITTY
LOUD	BULIMIC	CONVICT
DEAF	ANEMIC	HUNCHBACK
BLIND	MORMON	TEACHA'
LOST	DISABLED	SUBSTITUTE TEACHA'
VILE	NEARSIGHTED	SOULJA'
DUTCH	CLUBFOOTED	SISTA'
CZECH	SCOLIOSIS HAVIN'	COUZIN
NORSE	UNSYMPATHETIC	BOO

STEP #2: Concoct a clever way to combine all three parts of your rap name into one nonsensical, hard-to-pronounce word.

For Example:

If your name is: Po' Inappropriate Plebeian
Your clothing line should be called: Pöinnple

If your name is: Big Mormon Chiropracta'
Your clothing line should be called: Bimo-Chir

Hott Tip!: Add random accents, apostrophes, hyphens, and umlauts for effect!

STEP #3: Find a spokesmodel. The key to marketing your own clothing line is to have yourself in the ads. If you're ugly, compensate by showing lots of cars. If you're pretty, make sure that you're naked in the ad. If you're neither, contact Jackée's (of *227* fame) agent at (324) 555-4536.

STEP #4: Expand your clothing line by starting a label just for dogs. As they always say, it's never too early to start your own doggy clothing line.

WUSS WUT: **Throwbacks = (thro-bax) n. pertaining to the past; historical items; archaeological evidence of crunkness; shoes and jerseys no longer available in mass retail.**

III. Doggystyle

Even though your dog can't talk, your dog's outfit can speak a thousand words. This does not, of course, mean you

Hott Tip!: If you're going to cap your dog's teeth, make sure to take them out at night so lil' homey don't choke.

have to spend thousands on canine pimp gear. If you are strapped for cash and production costs are high, you can

Hott Tip!: Though it's important to keep your pet in constant floss, don't give your dog too many expensive items, as dogs tend to lose things and are strangely oblivious to the value of gold and money.

transform your human clothes into doggy gear with a few cuts of the scissors and several runs through the dryer! You'll have teeny-weeny tracksuits in no time!

Paul E. Pimp Wordz of Wizdum: "If yo' throwback is blue, yo' dog's should be too!"

NAME DAT DOG:

BREED: **Ho-Dog**

CHARACTERISTICS: **Poops. Barks. Humps other dogs.**

BREED: **Pimp-Dog**

CHARACTERISTICS: **Poops. Barks. Bitches love him.**

BREED: **Gangsta-Dog**

CHARACTERISTICS: **Poops. Barks. Loves gats. Is in a gang.**

BREED: **Baller-Dog**

CHARACTERISTICS: **Poops. Barks. Good at fetching.**

AMANDA McCALL & ALBERTINA RIZZO

BREED: Mogul-Dog

CHARACTERISTICS: Poops. Barks. Gets into all the VIP kennels.

BREED: Crack-Dog

CHARACTERISTICS: Poops. Occasionally eats his own poop. Smokes crack with owner.

IV. JEWELZ: DON'T MEAN A THING IF IT AIN'T GOT DAT BLING

"Feels like a midget is hanging from my necklace!"

—LUDACRIS

In the hip-hop world, to be bling-less is to be hopeless, and you, as a white girl, need all the help you can get. Having at least four to five pounds of jewelry on your body at all times is as necessary as having arms.* Remember, when it comes to crunk jewelry, it's not quality, it's quantity and density.

* For those readers who might argue that arms are not necessary, we ask you this: How easy is it to pour a bottle of Cristal with your feet while sitting naked in a Jacuzzi?

Basic Crunk Medallions:

➤ money sign

➤ gun

➤ bottle of Cristal

➤ cross

➤ Jesus on cross

➤ Jesus on cross with money sign

➤ Jesus on cross with money sign, gun, and bottle of Cristal

Cheaper Alternatives: All of the following items can be found in your own home and, with a little gold paint and a BeDazzler, can be transformed into crazy nice ice.

- a carving knife

- a garlic press

- pruning shears

- a whisk

- your "Most Improved
  Swimmer" Award (1987)
  from Sacajawikanaga
  Summer Camp

Caution: Wearing chains with the medallions mentioned
above may result in serious neck injury. Consult a
chiropractor if you plan to floss heavy-medal every day.

DO-IT-YOURSELF ICE

DIAMONDS: FRONT LIKE YO' CANARY IS REAL Nothing says hip-hop quite like canary diamonds, but real ones can be awfully costly. Here are some tips on turning your wack CZ (cubic zirconia) into a crunk canary.

1 Use a yellow highlighter to color your CZ.*

Because highlighter ink is not permanent, the color may rub off. To prevent embarrassment, carry around at least one highlighter at all times for retouching.

2 Soak in pineapple- or lemonade-flavored Kool-Aid overnight.*

May need to resoak several nights a week to maintain maximum floss.

GOLD: If you're like us, the Tiffany jewelry case you got for your sweet sixteen is probably filled with silver Elsa Peretti hearts, pearl earrings, fimo-bead bracelets, and a variety of hemp necklaces. Instead of viewing these items as evidence of your whiteness, you can transform them into proof of your crunkness in just four easy steps!

1   Take all your jewelry out of its case and place it on a cookie sheet.

2   Spray paint everything gold.

3   Let it dry.

4   Put it on.

Hott Tip!: If you can't afford to cap your teeth gold and you have a special event to go to, simply apply gold paint marker to your teeth. Be sure not to close your mouth or swallow, as paint markers can be toxic if ingested and can cause skin irritations!

V. Furz

We can all agree that hurting animals for their fur is bad, but fake fur simply will not fly in hip-hop circles.

For a quick and painless fur garment, just tranquilize your grandmother's Himalayan and wear it around your neck for the night. No one will know the difference!

Hott Tip!: If your grandma doesn't have a Himalayan, an alley cat will do just fine. Dogs, hamsters, and pigeons, however, are a no-no!

VI. CHAPTER EXERCISES

1 *Which of the following is NOT a safe way to dye your dog's fur to match your outfit?*

  A. KOOL-AID.

  B. FOOD COLORING.

  C. HENNA.

  D. CAR ENAMEL.

2 *Which of the following should you never give your dog to hold?*

    A. A BONE.

    B. A TENNIS BALL.

    C. A SQUEAKY TOY.

    D. A LOADED GUN.

3 *Which of the following products should not be marketed as part of your hip-hop empire?*

    A. BULLETPROOF VESTS.

    B. PLASMA SCREEN TVs.

    C. PASTIES.

    D. TEA COZIES.

4 *Which of the following is NOT an acceptable style for your dog?*

A. A DOG IN A FUR COAT.

B. A DOG IN A BIKINI.

C. A DOG IN A THONG.

D. A NAKED DOG.

ANSWER KEY: All answers are *D*, as in *Da Answer*.

DROP IT LIKE IT'S HOT:
Dance Tips & Social Etiquette

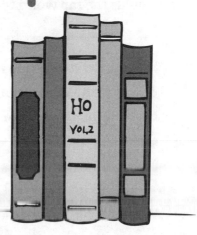

I. How to Be a Video Ho or Just Look Like One

Due to feminist seminars at universities and propagandist literature by Gloria Steinem, many white girls have been brainwashed into thinking that being a ho is somehow a "bad" thing.

The truth is, being a ho *is* bad . . . if you're really, really wack!

However, if you long to be crunk, you *must* embrace ho-dom in all its seminude glory, for the ho is the very glue that holds the rap world together.

> ## Hott Tip!: Undress to impress: Do not bring extra clothes to the video shoot. If you are going to bring anything, bring your own pole. It will increase your camera time and cut the video's budget in half.

HO-STORY: DA HIZTORY OF HOES

For years, scholars have pondered one seemingly insurmountable question: Which came first, the rapper or the ho? One thing's for sure, without hoes, rappers would have no one to gyrate on the hood of their Cadillac Escalades.

DA HO BEFO' DA VIDEO:

Call them muses, models, or mistresses, the women who inspired some of the greatest artists of all time were hoes. If Mona Lisa were alive today she'd be shaking her ass in a thong. Dante's Beatrice would've been nothing more than a bitch in a Jacuzzi. Hoes have been around for centuries,

but it was not until the invention of the rap video that hoes blossomed into what would become the greatest ho of all: the Video Ho.*

To further understand the development of a video ho, see figure below.

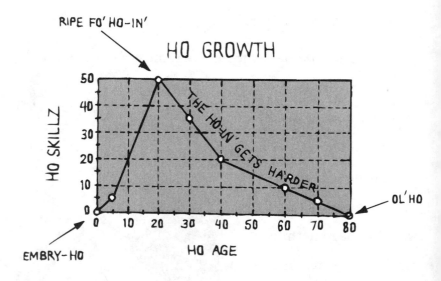

RIPE FO' HO-IN'

HO GROWTH

HO SKILLZ

THE HO-IN' GETS HARDER

EMBRY-HO

HO AGE

OL' HO

VIDEO HO MUST-HAVES:

1 GREEZINESS IS GODLINESS: BODY LUBRICANTS

As with any job, it is important that you come prepared for your work as a video ho. You must always be professional, and, in hip-hop terms, this means being well-lubed. The following is a list of lubricants that will keep you greezy fo' sheezy!

- Baby oil

- Crisco

- Vaseline

- Pam (for a ho on da go!)

- Sesame/Walnut/Peanut oil (for vegetarians!)

- Butter

- Paul Newman's Balsamic Vinagrette Dressing

Hott Tip!: Do not substitute with fat-free dressings and/or lo-cal/low-fat/lo-cholesterol spreads. Margarine will not appear greezy on camera.

PAUL E. PIMP'S WORDZ OF WIZDUM:
"A ho is a ho, quoth da raven, neva' mo'."

- Motor oil (Careful! Highly flammable but, when applied in a safe environment, can help achieve tanned, greezy-fresh look!)

Hott Tip!: Always wear heels that are at least eight inches high. (If you can't walk, no problem! Your role in the video will most likely only require that you either lie down or gyrate in place!)

2 WHORE-D'ŒUVRES: ORAL ACCESSORIZING

It is very important to insert phallic/erotic food items into your mouth whilst gyrating. Remember to practice beforehand; choking to death is *not* sexy. The following exercises will test your knowledge of oral accessories.

---

1 *Whilst gyrating in a video, which of the following items should be in your mouth?*

    A. A KEYTAR.

    B. GAFFING TAPE.

    C. SHREDDED WHEAT.

    D. A POPSICLE.

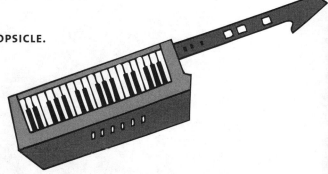

2 *The most hazardous thing to put in your mouth is*

A. A GAS PUMP.

B. URANIUM.

C. ANYTHING ON FIRE.

D. THE BARREL OF A RAPPER'S LOADED AK-15.

> **Hott Tip!**: Finger-licking is always sexy, but remember, the finger must be attached to the hand of a rapper. (No bloody stumps!)

BONUS QUESTION:

3 *Identify which wack person has been a video ho:*

    A. JENNIFER LOVE HEWITT.

    B. SARAH MICHELLE GELLAR.

    C. LISA MARIE PRESLEY.

    D. RUDY FROM *THE COSBY SHOW*.

    E. CHEVY CHASE.

    F. ALL OF THE ABOVE.

> **ANSWER KEY** All answers are *D*,
> as in *Da Answer*, except when da answer is *F*.

AMANDA McCALL & ALBERTINA RIZZO

3 THINGS TO HOLD: PROPS THAT'LL GIVE YOU PROPS!

Holding something while gyrating can transform you from a regular video ho into a video ho who's holding something! The following chart is meant to help you compare and contrast items that you should and should not hold.

HOLD	DON'T HOLD
Pimp cup	#1 Dad coffee mug
Bucket full of soapy water	Bucket full of baby turtles
Fur	Live mink
Shotgun	Rape whistle
Snake	Jar of mealworms

HOLD	DON'T HOLD
Pit bull	Seeing-eye dog
Another ho on a leash	Toddler attached to child safety harness

4 THINGS TO SIT ON: Put Yo' Ass into It

Studies show that while video hoes spend 60 percent of their camera time gyrating, they spend the remaining 40 percent sitting on or in something. The following chart shows what and what not to sit on or in.

SIT ON/IN	DON'T SIT ON/IN
Bathtub	Toilet
Giant pimp cup	Giant Stanley Cup
Sand	Wet asphalt
Rapper's face	Rapper's mom's face

AMANDA McCALL & ALBERTINA RIZZO

II. Dance Step Diagram

A. TORSO

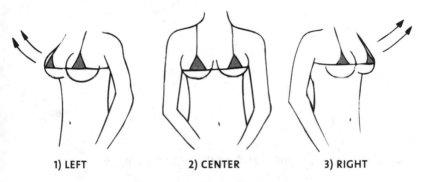

1) LEFT   2) CENTER   3) RIGHT

Continue to shake vigorously whilst performing steps 1, 2, and 3.

B. BUTTOCKS

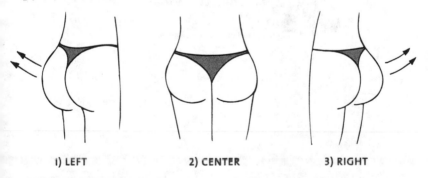

1) LEFT   2) CENTER   3) RIGHT

Continue to shake vigorously whilst performing steps 1, 2, and 3.

C. LEG-SPREADING

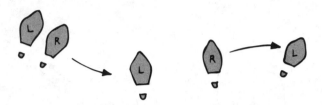

Combine Steps A, B, and C and repeat until it's a wrap!

III. Fill in da Blanx: Inspirational Club Stories

In this section, please select the appropriate words from the list below to complete the following story.

Da club	Da knee-cap
Bikini	Bitch-slappin'
Crunk	Shit
Cristal	Dat ho
Gat	Da club
Twenty-seventh	Crunk
Bitch	Hennessy
Front	Fuck
Shoot	Pistol-whipped

Bridget went to _____ and wore her favorite _____. She spent the whole night getting _____ on _____ and waving around her _____. After her _____ drink, another _____ started _____-ing. Bridget became very angry and proceeded to _____ her in _____. After _____ the _____ out of _____, Bridget went back to _____ and continued getting _____ on _____. That night, everyone learned a valuable lesson: If you _____ with Bridget, you're going to get _____.

SNOOP SEZ: **"Bitches ain't shit!"**

IV. Ask Paul E. Pimp

Here, world-renowned hustla' Paul E. Pimp, a Playaz Ball "Pimp of the Year Award" recipient nine years in a row, shares helpful advice on everything from social etiquette to gardening.

Dear Paul E. Pimp,

It's barely February in Kentucky and my tulips are a few inches tall. I'm concerned that the cold will kill them before spring. What should I do?

Heather

Frankfort, KY

Yo, Heather,

Girl, da only thing yo' two-lips should be doin' is sippin' on Cristal. And anotha' thing ... Lips can't die! Bitch, you CRAZY!

Dear Paul E. Pimp,

I'm obsessed with The Lord of the Rings. *I have the sound track, visit Web sites, and have read all of the books twice. The problem is that sometimes I get depressed because the whole thing is made up. Help!*

Elizabeth

Santa Barbara, CA

Yo, Elizabeth,

Girl, don't be depressed. Da lord of da rings is as real as the gems on my pimp cup. He works in New York on Forty-seventh and Sixth. Now, I'll admit, I had no idea Jacob da Jeweler had written any books, but big-ups fo' bein' a true fan of da man. Neva' give up, girl. Jacob's magic is real.

Dear Paul E. Pimp,

My parents are both in their forties and I'm beginning to worry about their health. They are both at least twenty to thirty pounds overweight and have high cholesterol. What can I do to encourage them to start exercising and eating healthier without hurting their feelings?

Jenny

Rosedale, Toronto

Canada

Yo, Jenny,

Girl, how yo' parents git in their forties? Da most I ever fit in a forty ounce was my toe, an' I ain't even fat! Damn, girl, yo' parents is CRAZY!

Dear Paul E. Pimp,

I am one of your most loyal readers and a great admirer of your pimping skills, but I've been noticing that you really struggle with homophones—words that sound alike but have different meanings. I was wondering if you've ever considered some kind of remedial education? If you're interested, I could suggest some excellent English-as-a-Second-Language courses for adults.

Polly,

Jackson Hole, WY

Yo, Polly,

A homophone! Girl, I ain't gay! Da only calls I git on my phone is from hoes. I got so many bitches, people think I own a kennel! I got a heterosexual-sex-o-phone an' it's always ringin' off da hook! Bitch, why you trippin'?

8 DAILY AFFIRMATIONS: Words of Wizdom from Yo' Favorite Rappers

The following is a small collection of some of our favorite quotations from today's hottest and wisest rappers. Read them whenever you need advice, comfort, or a little inspiration. We realize that maintaining crunkness is a day-to-day struggle. You will continue to encounter wack obstacles that will challenge your crunkness, leaving you frought with a variety of complex emotions. The following words of wisdom are like big warm hugs, self-help tools that will enable you to overcome any obstacle and continue in your journey through Crunkville.*

"Love money, hate haters."

—MASTER P.

"Fuck you, Fuck you, Fuuuuuuuuuuuuuuuuuuuuuuuuuucccccccck yoooooooooou."

—CAM'RON

"A bitch is a bitch."

—Ice Cube

"When I'm representin' my city, I'm suckin' on a bitch titty."

—C-Murder

"Money make the world go round, so let's get mo'."

—Young Buck

"Playas wanna play, ballas wanna ball, rollas wanna roll."

—R. Kelly

"Bitches ain't shit."

—SNOOP DOGG

"The cash money motto we got to drink 'til we throw up."

—CASH MONEY MILLIONAIRES

"Don't take 'em to the club unless they bonin'."

—NOTORIOUS B.I.G. FEATURING TOO $HORT

"Fuck da police."

—ICE CUBE

"U at the bar (Get drunk)

U in ya car (Get crunk)."

—BIG POKEY FEATURING CHRIS WARD

"You can't be Baby!"

—BABY OF CASH MONEY MILLIONAIRES

"Murder ain't nuttin' but a misdemeanor."

—Lil Wayne featuring Mannie Fresh

"The baby doesn't look like me."

—K-Solo

"Who let these hoes in my room? (Did you let 'em in?)
Who let these hoes in my room? (I need to know,
who let these hoes in?)"

—Ludacris

"All we do is smoke and just so you know
My motto is fuck you bitch and fuck a ho."

—Kurupt

"We the sharks in the water, y'all popcorn shrimps
So you can eat my cocktail sauce and ass!"

—Anybody Killa featuring Jamie Madox

"Yo Boo-Tee

Yo Boo-Hoo-Tee

Yo Boo-Tee

Yo Boo-Hoo-Hoo-Hoo-Tee."

—R. KELLY

"I don't love you, ho, I'm out the do'."

—SNOOP

"You remind me of my jeep."

—R. KELLY

"You're nothin' but a stank ho' tryin' to take my bank ho'."

—N.W.A.

"You ain't from Russia so girl why you rushin'?"

—NELLY

"The way you do the things you do

reminds me of my Lexus Coupe."

—R. Kelly

"Money, cash, hoes.

Money, cash, hoes."

—Jay-Z

"Shut the fuck up."

—Eazy-E

* If, as times goes on, you find that you are losing your crunkness and giving in to wack temptations, have no fear. *Hold My Gold: A White Girl's Guide to the Hip-Hop World, Volume II: The Saga Continues*, a.k.a. *Tha Return of tha Gold*, a.k.a. *HMG: Da Family Dynasty*, a.k.a. *La Bella Donna Bianca, Tha Sequel*, a.k.a. *We Back Fo' Mo'*, a.k.a. *Did We Mention We Back?* a.k.a. *Big Publishin'*, a.k.a. *Still Publishin'*, a.k.a. *Part II: We Done It Again*, a.k.a. *HMG Second Edition: Bigga 'n' Crunka*, a.k.a. *HMG: Tha Resurrection*, a.k.a. *The Divine Crunkedy II*, a.k.a. *Crunkering Heights II*, a.k.a. *Tha Catcher in tha Crunk II*, a.k.a. *Webster's English Crunk-o-nary II*, a.k.a. *The Koran-ka-dunk II* will be droppin' soon at a bookstore near you.

Diploma

This certifies that _____

has satisfactorily completed the course of study

prescribed by Hold My Gold: A White Girl's Guide

to the Hip-Hop World, *and, having met the*

requirements for graduation, is entitled to

this diploma in Crunkness.

ALBERTINA RIZZO

AMANDA McCALL

PEACIN' OUT: SHOUT OUTS!

We couldn't have done this without the help of one O.G.: Our man Jesus (a.k.a. Da Creata', a.k.a. J-Dawg, a.k.a. God's Son, a.k.a. Da Messiah.) We also gots 2 give mad luv 2 Mr. Simon (a.k.a. Simyson, a.k.a. Big Sim, a.k.a. Sim-Sima) and Mr. Schuster (a.k.a. Schu-Dog, a.k.a. Wut Schu lookin' at?, a.k.a. Sharp Schu-tah). Mad respect 2 Willy-Will "Da Literary Agent" Clark, You'z a real pimp at gettin' contrax! Nanda "Da Otha' White Meat" Murray, U make editing look like diamonds! Albertina gots ta give mad love 2: Alberto "my true hero" Rizzo, Cristina "da mom" Rizzo, Jevon "Da one true luv" Roush, Paolo "Big P NYC" Rizzo, Christian "Lil' Baby" Rizzo, Mark "Marky Mark" Roskans, Robin "Lil Rob" Narvaez, Reyna, Tessa "Tezzzz" Roush, Caitlin "Whatchu talkin' 'bout"

Roush, Kathryn "Da 2nd momma" McAuliffe, Jay "Da consigliere" Kriegel, Ali "Da new baby mama + B.F.F." Grimes, Steph "Keepin' it real" Cozzi, Jessica "Fairy crunk mother" Koslow, Connor "Sean John" Kriegel, Isabel "lil' Iz" Kriegel, Liza "Crazy legs" Rodriguez, Elizabeth "Kneel on deez" Neel, Martin "Pneu" Smith, Grandma, Big Unc + Auntie Amieva + Lil' Cuzinz too, the Segneurs, + all da otha' fams and da Posen Posse. Amanda gots ta give mad luv 2: Bruce "Brucey-Bruce" McCall (a.k.a. Da Crunkinator, a.k.a. Big Papa, a.k.a. Big Daddy B., a.k.a. B-Diddy Combs) + Polly "Polly-Pol" McCall, My #1 cuz Max "Uh-Oh Oreo" Holihan (U my inspiration, dawg. Mad love. Keep pimpin'!), Ginny "Gin & Juice" Holihan, Graciela, Neal, + Lil' Marley Meltzer, Floyd "Da Cat" McCall (Meow, dawg!), Smit "Ready fo' Shit" Reddy, Helen Millah-Killah, Wack Waxman, Joey Sayre, K-2-da-mutha-fuckin'-T Friedman, Brien "Da Brain" Kelley, B-Ro, Chris Ann + Ricky fo' da crunk crib, Da Letterman Crew, David Rakoff, Sarah B., Krissie Mc-G., Nightingale-Bamford, University of Wisconsin + Connecticut College (for helping me 2 understand whiteness). Amanda & Albertina also gots ta thank da following products + people so as 2 perhaps get some endorsements + free food +/or otha' stuff: peanut butter (not chunky cause chunky is real wack), a variety of cheeses (we love U goat!), Zone bars (U keep our calories in check), Diet Coke with Lime (U mad refreshin'), Chinese food (I ain't mad at cha), Mexican (U also real good but them refried beans need more time in da oven . . . check yo'self!) Water (specifically Fiji: U taste better than real water!), Nike: we don't have any of U, but we like U: We are sizes 8.5 + 10.5. Cookie dough: U real raw! Marshmallow fluff: Even though Amanda dissed U, U will always be in Albertina's heart. Cadbury Creme eggs: What's yo' problem? How come I can only find U durin' Easter time . . . U got a problem with otha' religions? U should chill + be sold all year round. Bread, U are the vehicle dat get da cheese in my mouth . . . U also good with peanut butter too! Mozzarella balls: U are one special dairy product. Milk, U help make mozzarella balls. The Source, Vibe, XXL, B.E.T., Dave Chapelle, Larry David, the whole G-Unit Crew, David Blaine (yo' magic is real). 2 our bling: Keep blingin', baby! Biggie R.I.P., Tupac R.I.P., thanks fo' da memories . . . + 2 all da otha' rappers who may not be with us by the time this book drops, R.I.P. in advance. Ludacris, U put da ass back in class. Cristal, U make our dreams come true. Can we drink U in da morning too? Nelly, U seem real nice: My parents want 2 meet U. Trick Daddy, 2 be honest, U real scary: My parents said U wasn't allowed ova' . . .

Sorry, dawg! Jane Austen: da baddest bitch. Vladimir Nabokov: fo' keepin' us crunkski. Bentley, can we drive U, like, everyday? Also, can we not pay fo' U? Apples, U keep the docta' away. Big ups 2 milk, again, featuring cereal + coffee. Italy, "*Andiamo al cinema, bitches!*," Bone Crusha, RZA, + GZA: Thanks fo' da care packages. CP-Dub Crew, da So-Hos. Diamonds, can we have U? Dan Rather, U crazy! Humidifier, U bust a cap in my allergies. Squirrels, can I get a nut? 2 my neck + ears: U hold my bling. Toenails, my feet would look mad crazy without U! The guy from Survivor 2 (Panama) wit da brown hair who got kicked out fo' failin' da challenge . . . dat wuz wrong dawg . . . why did they kick U out of tribal council . . . that otha' bitch should've been voted out, + fuck Jeff Probst, he a pussy anyway! 2 those little things at da end of my shoelaces: What are U called? Baby rabbits, why U so cute? Da environment, sorry fo' fuckin' wit U, U be aiight though! Cockroaches + rats, we don't like U! Sharks + adult bears, U scare us. Thumbs: U keep monkeys in check. Pimples, why U always gotta show up befo' a big daylike dat time when I had 2 go 2 meet my friend + she had anotha' friend who was cute + U showed up + I tried 2 dry U wit toothpaste but it didn't work so I tried coverin' U up + then people axed me if I had a cold sore . . . remember dat shit!? Da East Side

Boyz: Can U give us advice on how 2 meet Lil Jon? Snoop, is pimpin' really easy? I think it might be hard . . . discuss amongst yo'selves. Cats: Some of U are real vindictive. Google: I hate librarians, so I'm real glad U exist . . . thanks fo' da 411, although I did Google "deez nuts" under "Images" + U didn't have nuthin . . . update yo' system, biatch! Post-It notes: One time I tried 2 go 2 a party wit U + write offensive things like "I'm real stupid + wack" or "My mamma is a bitch" or "Shoot me in da face" or "Stick yo' ass in my face + fart" or "Kick me in da privates" or "Spit in my food" or "Burp + then blow the air in my face" or "Send me a computer virus + fuck up all my shit" on U so that I could stick U on otha' people's bax, but yo' glue don't stick too good, so I had 2 go home + get some Scotch tape, but by the time I got back, da party was ova' . . . why they call it Scotch tape anyway? Dat shit Scottish? It wear a kilt? Kilts are fo' bitches. Coffee, U are aromatic + romantic. Also, thank U 2 chairs: Our asses is mad grateful. Finally, a big up 2 God, for inventing chairs.

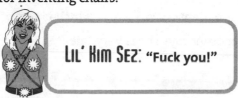

LIL' KIM SEZ: "Fuck you!"

About Da Authors

ALBERTINA RIZZO grew up in the trenches of SoHo. She has worked as an editor for *Seventeen* and *New Woman* magazines, and most recently as Public Relations Director for designer Zac Posen. Ms. Rizzo enjoys creating shoebox dioramas, doing crossword puzzles, and committing grand larceny. In the fall of 2004, she thought she saw P. Diddy running the NYC marathon from Amanda McCall's parents' window. She is currently a full-time author (or, as her mother puts it, "lazy").

AMANDA McCALL has worked for *The New Yorker* and *The Late Show with David Letterman*. She enjoys Jenga tournaments, baking, and robbin' people. In the summer of 2003, she saw Lil' Kim at a Yankees game eating nachos. Amanda grew up on the mean streets of Central Park West, which is sort of near the Bronx. Her mother says she is very talented.